MOBILE

MOBILE

Tanis MacDonald

Book*hug Press
Toronto

The production of this book was made possible through the generous
assistance of the Canada Council for the Arts and the Ontario Arts Council.
Book*hug Press also acknowledges the support of the Government of Canada
through the Canada Book Fund and the Government of Ontario through the
Ontario Book Publishing Tax Credit and the Ontario Book Fund.

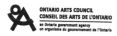

ONTARIO
CREATES | ONTARIO
CRÉATIF

Book*hug Press acknowledges the land on which it operates. For thousands of
years it has been the traditional land of the Huron-Wendat, the Seneca, and
most recently, the Mississaugas of the Credit River. Today, this meeting place is
still the home to many Indigenous people from across Turtle Island, and we
are grateful to have the opportunity to work on this land.

Library and Archives Canada Cataloguing in Publication

Title: Mobile / Tanis MacDonald.
Names: MacDonald, Tanis, author.
Description: Poems.
Identifiers: Canadiana (print) 20190157712 | Canadiana (ebook)
     20190163046 ISBN 9781771665308 (softcover) | ISBN 9781771665315
     (HTML) ISBN 9781771665322 (PDF) | ISBN 9781771665339 (Kindle)
Classification: LCC PS8575.D6657 M63 2019 | DDC C811/.54—dc23

Printed in Canada

For my mother, who never learned to drive
(*miss you like crazy*)

TABLE OF CONTENTS

We walk. The city unfolds its blocks.
The sidewalk loves our feet to a pulp,
our blisters watery as eyes, but better
that a woman should walk these streets
than make one's own vicinity a cattle
chute, a gauntlet to be run. Better that
women should be seen and not hurt.
If thine eye offend thee, Baudelaire,
cluck it out. My corns elude
legibility. Street haunter, following
the thicks and thins. Empty
lots, ellipses: scare optics, gnaw ledge.

We were just walking,
Officer. We were following desire lines.
          Flâneuse-moi,
c'est le nom propre, allons-y,
le mot juste, la moue justesse,
langue and parole me. Hey,
I'm walking here.

          Fleuve, Philomela.
Reversed bird, swallow as
nightingale, nightingale
as lark, as starling. Invasive
species of a thousand tongues,
river the city. Reverse the sieve order
and see what flows. Not gonna lie:
walking's dicey, but so's the bus.
How spatial our practices, how
mobile our units. Where
will we walk? Even the tallest
letters in the world crumble.

1. SYBIL ELEGIES

ELEGY 1

In the city I long for, women
repleat their origins. We do not
eke out evenings courting in parks.
The light does not ride
easy on us all. If only
we could learn not to love
meaning before we make it.
If only our ache
could arc like metal
in a microwave. If only
our exemplar was more
tectonic than catatonic.
Don't mind me. I throe
like a girl, cacophony's
blasted cadence. It's hard
to undo the centre when your
absence is
invisible.

*

Ai Weiwei's *Moon
Chest*, like the Cabinet of
Dr. Caligari, will show you
all the phases if you
bend to look. Don't be
distracted
by the texture of the
quince
wood. Don't be distracted by
the word *quince*. (Not *quints*,
though this is Canada.) It's okay
if you squint. This is not
like shopping for a bedroom set
or agony.

I don't like it, she says, and
wants me to agree. I point
through the cut-outs to the phases
ordered as a fanned deck. She won't
even pretend to look
until I walk between
phases, a body dividing wood,
then she gasps
(I am nearly invisible though not
yet silver) *you're the woman
in the moon!*

Let me perch on the rim of my
crater, your friendly neighbourhood
menstrual symbol, footsore and
ready to spit, Diana's arrow back
from the Sea of Crises
for a homecoming

between heaven and concrete. The city
will be judged and found
wanting, one more
way to say a woman's
body is neither null
nor void, of course. The moon
is always in transit.

*

The café's circus with
bread: the boy
with his camera, the stoner
staggering beneath
the weight of three bags
full, sir,
the girl in the purple Joy
Division T-shirt, the handsome
man smoking on the patio like
his drop-dead
life depends on the plume
lofting from his firm bottom
lip, curled pout checking
his status—still
not satisfied. The great minds of his
generation hysterical on
grande extra-hot latte, naked
in Gore-Tex. Say
he's smoked the official
dope before and after
it was legal and excited universal
admiration for his keen
grasp of the obvious. Say
those hipsters are angle-headed,
acute. Say the café has wait
staff younger than my
pants. They practise the kind
efficiency of trained
millennials, not eaten away by
the history we did not care
to know even as it hooked
and dragged us. Say then, we
who used to walk here, who stalked
these bricks, played it loose,
uncertain of our footing, led on by
swamp gas, foxfire
bravado.

ELEGY 2

I'd like to
thank the brave women
of this city for reminding
me fine ironic throes
aren't worth the bubble wrap
they came in. My newsfeed
says in Canada, a woman is
assaulted every fifteen minutes.
I believe it
down to the number
and frequency of
chases and scrapes and
oh come ons I heard the years
I could not reach
up to the poverty line, when
riding the subway was for
special occasions and I walked
the twenty blocks home from
my closing shift at 2:00 a.m.
because every dollar was too
hard to earn
to waste it on safety.
I know the dead
women persist, but not
through these bylaws.
I believe it
down to the number
of names and frequencies
on which we receive advice (Delta
Oscar November Tango) to stay in,
better to void
the scandal of being
than to call ourselves
bloodied, call ourselves
heroes by any other means.

*

I come from the place
beside the place
beneath the radar
those long
suburban blocks
in January dark
walking home with my skates
over my shoulder and
thinking of how fast a skate blade
sharpened that morning
would go through a neck
and I knew just the neck
and you knew him too
and you laughed at his jokes
so don't mistake me
for a girl who doesn't
know don't
think l am not
alive and counting
who died
walking home
from the store
or their part-time job
in the winter dark
don't idle your car by me
don't lean over the passenger seat
and say *hey, get in*
all I need is me
thanks I don't
want your kind
of lift

*

Call me a foot soldier
in an unregistered
army of young women walking
home from dirty jobs, grey
with grease, taking back
the night by ourselves
and not talking about
the skirted
subject
of cab fare.
It was rumoured among us
as a law never upheld
or even tested
that if you worked
late enough your boss was
legally bound to pay
for your cab home but no matter
how late I worked this never
happened though we repeated
this fake statute
among ourselves
and waited for those last
few
tables
to leave. Those
years, and every year,
someone was paid
much more than me
to remind me of
my job.

*

we roll forward dull
as tanks you shod us
you tipped us
you grimed us
you would not
notice a phalanx of your
servers and cleaners
on foot on the street
a regiment of working
class girls caught in
your rear-view
mirror we are
not even vanishing
points as you hit
the on-ramp
to the expressway
to the suburbs
and we flip
you the bird so many
times it looks like
a flock of seagulls
lifting our hands
up and away

ELEGY 3

the rules

never take the TTC after midnight
never live downtown

sui generis
we are all individuals together
never go to the park alone
if someone follows you, let your teeth chatter
he might believe you are someone

habeas corpus
never make eye contact
if he whistles
if he says he loves you
if he makes kissy sounds
you have the body
you are a citizen

dux femina facti
never go north of Eglinton
or to Scarborough
or to High Park
and never live
downtown
never live alone
never breathe alone
trust no one
especially old television slogans
the brute is out there
lead as you have been
followed

*

Cheap shoes did my back
no favours. Walking made me
suspect and available to
you've got to be kidding.
The city ushered me past
houses sleek with creams and
powders and carved
salad bowls and
other people's parents who
tossed the lettuce
just so. Lordly and masterly,
the city demanded my bone
scrapings every night.

When I read that walking
was a scholarly position,
that men understood
the city from their
strolls, I drew breath
(not for the first
time) to say *you can't have it
both ways.*

*

get your ear to the ground
this grassy hill
gets you down
to hear screams of women
beneath the green

as you are passing through
through passing as you are

beneath the green
screams of women
down you get to
here this grassy ear
to the getting ground

*

if you turn your ankle on
an angle turn it into
a virtue or turn it down

stretch stirrup
wrap bone
sculpt arch

that's a hallucis blunder
anatomy's bonenote
you'd better

toe the line
until your foot swells
put the pain in sprain

the distal fibula
knows where you livula

ELEGY 4

He shakes my hand
at the party and tugs me
toward him, whispers
I like your accent. I don't know
why it's a secret, or why
it's an accent. He heard
in my vowels the town
my mother was born in.

There are places where
being born three hundred
miles away
makes anyone a barbarian
despite global citizenship
so I say thank you with
my prairie accent, putting
the Turtle Mountains and the
General Strike behind
the words, and say it for

the professor who said
*I wish you were more
urbane,* for all the times
my mother refused to speak
in public, for my grandmother's
twitching upper lip,
for the nuisance
grounds. Tug him close

and whisper *By our
fucking working-class accents
you shall goddamn know us.*

*

The impress of our bleeding
bodies did not crush the ivy
climbing the stone walls
of universities we would never
attend because we could not
imagine them, though I met
plenty of pocket
mouths who spoke like
they owned the museum, grew up
playing knucklebone with
the femurs kept in the
drawers.

That's so pedestrian.

If you are born with a silver
tongue in your ear, you accept
latitude as your due.

*

My grandfather lived in a boxcar
for the bleak year of 1923,
and when he said *my job*, he never
expected to feel clean. I knew how
to clean silver, but not buy it. I passed
beneath those serpent-topped gates
one night with an Upper Canada
Boy and thought I heard
the click of tumblers
aligning on numbers,
the chock and clunk of fate
and hard work made hand-fast
at last. All this could be
mine, would line up at my feet
if I just divined the combination,
or if I could, like poor girls
everywhere,
wish it open.

*

I tried to want it and
could not wish though professions
of love issued from a foot
above my head and I
heard only desire tarted
up as the future. The ravine
knew me better. It offered me
what I had always known:
the sound of scurrying and feet
running after prey. A girl's
gotta eat. She's gotta
put one foot in front.
She's gotta move like
she's made of
moving. She's gotta practise
with a raccoon's deft
hands, headfirst in the garbage.

*

who's the patron saint
of tired women? someone
who will deliver me
from old-Ontario stock with
their brilliant martyrs and
their stories about a nation's failure
of nerve, about how the Canadian
Shield would protect me from
the haunting of those exacting
spectres, about how they
pronounced for my own good
the ways the world would crush
the likes of me

*

on Philosopher's Walk, we
passed the statue of the crucified
woman, her arms stretched
wide and legs dangling—
rising or hanging, ascending
or dying? I knew when we walked by her
the Upper Canada Boy
would say *I'll bet*
you like that I'll bet you think
it's feminist and when I gave him
the flat-eyed *can it, buster,*
he followed with a reading from
his standard text: how I would never
understand transubstantiation or
Bertrand Russell. Oh boy: another lesson
in apostate politics. He warned me
against pronouncing
the *c* in autodidact. He was full
of good advice
I did not take.

ELEGY 5

the city was a bad
boyfriend when I was his
girl he called me
late to ask who I was
with when I was his girl he
talked forever about his
great future I
was the girl he
idled behind for
blocks tried to
pass me around
like a drag on
a cigarette girl on
the subway girl in the flat
shoes smart girl
spare girl left
girl right girl that
year's girl the girl who
said *I'm gone*

and the city said

oh come on
girl don't be
like that
I know what
you need

*

inspected like a package
before my shift by
a seventy-year-old man
(who was beloved by all
though he saved his hairy
eyeball for me)
whose job it was to see
if I was clean enough
to serve and when I was
by a slim
margin he growled
in my ear *this is business*
and kept an eye peeled for
stray hairs he could tell
by how I walked I was a spy
in the century house of
good grooming

*

There was sometimes trouble
on the late shift and then
there were bouncers
and sometimes blood. Our
daily grind of taking
the measure of empire and
serving it hot before divvying
up the damp and jingling
contents of the tip
jar didn't stop
guys we knew from
laughing on our nights off
about picking up
a drunk girl (like us),
taking her (like us) to his place,
and being back for last call (without us)
to howls of approval and songs
rewritten to brag:
if I can make her
there, I'll make her anywhere.

It was a no-win year strung with
quislings, friends
with broad skunk stripes down their
lissom backs, and one who
raised his sad eyes to me
men are just hard-wired
that way. Relax. Beware
the brides of March,
the long reach of
those toothy breeder
grins. The tongue must be
sure as shooting. Like us.

*

What? Did you
think I had
forgotten?
Time is an aunt who
looks at you like
she will send you back
like a defective coffeemaker
if you make one
wrong move.
Time's relative. Time's
riddled. How is a prairie
girl like an elephant?
She remembers
sure as shooting.

ELEGY 6

On this soapbox, on this
day, I come to open
the book of myths and call
winged furies down between
these benches and burned
zinnia beds. I always
have been one for
whom the world is too
much. I am a claxon
blaring I object
and subjected
I dare.

To be our own women! To own
our faces and thighs and the firmness
of our grip. What our mothers
gave up to teach us to stand. Sing
the names of our murdered sisters,
our missing and bartered selves, our
ripped children. Open
the book to Philomela; hear in
the voice of the shuttle my mother's
face when she stood tall in
her polyester Sears
separates and told
the UC Boy *my daughter
doesn't want to talk to you* and
cracked down
the receiver like she was killing
a cockroach. Turn
from the sink and walk out
the doors we sanded
and into the squirrel-surveyed

pigeon-bitten streets, mist
from the ravine rising
behind our heads as we sprout
wings and fan them out like
mandalas. We are
a city where Gwendolyn
MacEwen does not aspirate
on a sandwich while quitting cold
turkey alone in the Annex, where Isabella
Valancy Crawford does not starve
a stone's throw from the asylum, where
lunatic villas spill laughing
women and children with designs
for astounding bicycles, where girls walk
out of the ravine on strong
calves and know how to make a fist, where
the Necropolis glows with polish and
the scent of rice and peas wafts
over it, where llamas and donkeys
at Riverdale Farm smell
the deer in the ravine and
jump the fences at night
to frolic and return at dawn, half-wild
and pleased with their double lives,
where grassroots and roses grow on Jane
Jacobs's ladder

where our cadence is
not coincidence
or compliance
or concordance

where we do not eat imperial
humiliations, do not call them
necessities nor cook them

into meat pies for others, where
we save our laments for
those who died hard because the law
failed and failed and failed them.
Tear down the hoardings. Keen.

*

Sybilla, grey-trimmed with
roadkill, counts
small bodies courtesy of the long
commute. She washes her
ragged feet in Taddle Creek.
Philomela reads out nouns
and chooses to call them
new: condo, park, expressway,
market, girl on the subway.

Sister, citizen,
you farthest, you dearest, here
your humid body, your blistered
heels. You are the long will.
A woman is loosed from time by
how she will speak and be
spoken, by how she pays
daily in flames and high notes.
A siren's a boulevard of broken
memes. All those eggs,
beautiful blasted
stones.

2: JANE WALKS

William, I walk the city. You'd
call it Byzantium. It is no
country for young women; I know
why they are in one another's arms.

And me, makar, I walk the blocks
and louder sing. Jig when I can.
Fish or fowl, I'll take my form
from any natural thing

and more
besides, bespoke, begotten,
besotted. I'll take the sidewalk
test and pass

with flying colours. I'll rummage
in the marvellous
order. Give me a rundown building,
give me squatters; I'll show you

a woman's shawl in the weave
and colour of my skin.
Now that we are old and
grey and full of sleep, I'll say

an aged woman was never
a paltry thing. Gather me
into what is. To come,
makar. To see.

LUCKY JANE, LEAKY OBJECT

The city's no arcade, no gallery, no marketplace. I will grow
older on the sidewalk.

Bunions, pull cart, three layers of skirts, Leafs jersey beneath
cable-knit beneath cardigan beneath green cloth coat.
I'm as crazy as you. Or me.

I can slip you an aphorism if you're short. *Always stand your
broken ground* or *We are leaky as skin.*

Do not fear the hiss of the stars. Call me a citizen's cane, I'll
stamp your passport. I'll welcome you and your
luggage to this blister nation: river valley, park, hard
runnels of alleys, weedy community garden.

Have you anything to declare? Your public diagnosis. Your
basket of rotting apricots.

If you know me, raise your hand, your glass, your ruckus,
raise your interest rates.

Madwoman of the Danforth, every day on the corner across
from World of Cheese. Everyone sees me; no one does.

Practice makes suspect. If you lie down with dogs,
you get up at five. If you lie down with ducks,
you get up with down. For every polar bear,

a Wal-Mart greeter. In Chekhov,
mansplainers know their snuff. Buddy, you're
skating on thin splice. You're

shitting in the catbird seat. You're howling
at the loon. Nothing mud will come of this.
Don't say I didn't swarm you.

There's a suture torn every minute.

JANE IN TADDLE CREEK PARK

Up like a pigeon from the sewers! You can't
dam this into a pond. Casement protection
does the can-can. What rivulets fall, what
the creek composes: infinity wound, sleek mouse,
watershed ravine. Here she hisses
hawthorn berries; here realtors shudder to find
cowbirds in half-submerged basements,
famished, eating drywall. Here we pay
homage to the limits of erudition. Here
we interpolate echoes, and here call down
all citifying signs, here we stand
beneath the vessel overflowing with rain.
Here we lavish clay, muskrat, backhoe.

sleeps head on stone whole soul rent[1] brooks no
interferon a woman of mixed
address and your first best nighthag.
Jane's your aunt chained and smiling
suffrage your mother dumpster diving
Jane occupies soil mojo working that dynamically stable[2]
circus. If Jane fried out, who among
the furious order would not cry technopolis?[3] Jane's the scrub
poplars at the parking lot at No Frills[4] the cormorant
shit that's killing the trees Jane's thirsty believes
nothing dreams but it's free.[5] Jane's a fumbly
history of the knocks[6] Russian olive concrete and wild
cannot.[7] Jane's apocalypse as cross
word puzzle a small incessant push of the cardiac
legion[8] and she won't go on welfare because that's
only for people who are really
hard up.[9] Jane knows Ishpadinaa by the Spadina Line
Iroquois Furrow Survey Avenue Power Dairy Archive[10] scrupulous
seed folk hermetic Dame Jane Dirt Jane in the natural
ordure

1   W. B. Yeats, "Crazy Jane Talks with the Bishop."
2   Jane Jacobs, *Dark Age Ahead*
3   R. M. Rilke via Dennis Lee, *Civil Elegies*
4   Erín Moure, *A Sheep's Vigil by a Fervent Person*
5   Dionne Brand, *thirsty*
6   Meira Cook, *A Walker in the City*
7   Margaret Avison, *Concrete and Wild Carrot*
8   Dennis Lee, *Civil Elegies*
9   Gwendolyn MacEwen, "The Transparent Womb"
10 Brad Golden and Norman Richards, "Spadina Line"

JANE, ROVER

The state has no menopause, only productivity and loss.
—Lisa Robertson, "Proverbs of a She-Dandy"

She will consider
aging while the city slips.
She will consider
the twinge in her hips.
Jane's her own
spreadsheet, but she's no
fillable form. She will consider
productivity as a flu she
fought for years.

She will consider
the state on menopause, its
hot flash drives, its loss leaders.
The city dresses in layers.

When Jane was young,
the city taxed her lips, her eyes,
her dividend of thighs.
No good looks go unpunished.
She learned to bounce
off standards like
off a bumper.

Jane is a chatelaine with
the keys to nowhere,
she's rover, she's riever,
she's rougher. A woman whose
trade in trash
is brisk, whose office is
a picnic table

where someone is
always waiting for her
to leave, *geez*
you stink,
oh yes,
it's what a woman does under
the stars and her own power.

This is your Jane on menopause.
Any questions?

JANE'S NIGHTINGALE

When Jane is crowned the Queen
of Swords, she is not chastened: she's
no sister of mercy or torment.

She grasps the hilt in her potato-dirt
hand, beckons with the other.
The Queen of Swords knows a lie

when it rolls up and starts to rhumba.
She's never been one to slide away.
She knows the long tickertape

of deferred grief, sobbing nightingale
in an orchard dead by the highway.
Jane collects wrinkled apples on

the point of her sword.
If she offers you one, don't
hesitate.

How many miles the way the crow's feet
dig? Damp Babylon, uncoupled from

reproduction: sharp baby ain't no body's
crucial collective object.

Eats dirt, spits father, disperses dancers through
the Luminous Veil to spin above the Don.

Don't point that thing at me.
I don't need no stinking Garden of Eden.

Punk's an old woman with a kick like a mule's wish.
Basilisk baby shines up heteroglossia to a sleek

infidel polish, spirals down and blasphemes the steep
path to the ravine. Puzzle this

wrench from socket, chrome torso creaking wide
open. Snap baby's a sunshine-belt fog machine and organic

analogy, metal coyote with taut rivets and a knuckling
down deep to the now future cosmos.

Quintessence a woman's weatherskin.
Come here, chimera.

Jane's hardly to be seen
among the papers gleaned
from the apprentice mage.
She does not show her age.
He called her Cracked Mary
but Jane walks unhurried,
backed by the pic of Maud
Gonne, looking just, by God,
like she'd clean Willie's clock
in two short rounds: tick, tock.

Jane's the dyke offspring of the piano man's daughter's daughter. Jane floated down the 400 to land in Sibelius Park, she's the love child of Kip and Hannah, she's every girl lost on a Girl Guide trip who turned into a bear at the mouth of the Humber. Don't wag your finger to that cadence. This is a meeting of Jane's minds: buried river, fox crossing the valley, subway passing overhead. Jane's arch: she had love and land enough. She's crossing the bridge as it burns.

JANE'S WEATHER FORECAST

I'm a leather cloud and get anywhere from
forty to seventy years an hour. It's a hard

life if you don't deepen, but shelters
wall you in. They say the cold won't

get you if you keep moving but they don't know
squat. Cold keeps company. I've kept it myself.

I'll tell you what's crazy. I've both slept
on steps and taken millions. If you think

sprawl is the way to go you are
barking up the wrong me.

JANE'S HOUSE

She was young a whole person ago.
Jane used to sell insurance
and now she's a liability.

Jane slips on the riverbank
after rain, by the bridge.
Jane picks fiddleheads, but
can't tell good mushrooms
from bad. Jane lurks,
and good lurk to her. She builds
a house from stacks of
flood-swollen books.
Her house of refute.

What breaks a broker?
Fern wants to know.

Jane'd give you the skirt
off her back. She'd give you
mint she finds by the river though
didn't the woman with the grey
streaks in her hair, the one who makes
frybread for whoever shows up on Fridays
at the Kitchen on College, didn't she
snort when she told Jane
mint grows everywhere if you look?
(*Call me Fern* because she said
Jane couldn't pronounce her real

name and she didn't want
to hear
Jane try.) Fern knows what
grows where. She warns Jane
about giant hogweed and poison
ivy's plump white berries.
Fern tells Jane to spread her skirt
beneath the mulberry
tree. Fern says the river used to
wind, but they switched it to a new
channel. The river used to have more
salmon, but they were hit by
bricks, picked off one by one.

The sidewalk's never soft and the truth is
Jane stole for decades and is paying back
slowly: the settler installment plan,
anthropocene, obscene.

Chew this, says Fern.
Pick that. Smell. Swallow.
Lamb's quarters, pigweed:
it's all the same. Eat it
and you'll keep your teeth unless
someone knocks them out.

CROSS-STITCH SAMPLER FOR THE HOUSE OF REFUTE

Fury is a homing device.
Shrug like ordinary hell
is the address from which
you forward your mail.

step across this wavy line. limp across this leaving. Don was here.
oh yes, we had him up to here, high wide and handsome, kingfisher
in the restored pond when he sidled up to Danaë and she decked
him before he could make rain

Danu flows both ways baby better not forfeit

freshet turned river high on its own banking system, high on its
   own confidence
current, flood of trees who leapt into the wash, bridge following
   the swing,
its oxbow fluency, leaning willows, fast eddies and their cycles

noisy gnashing flows the Dôn

always floods to sweep bridges away
loosening struts swaying and bobbing cross me

river beast kept in the stone cage by the pond, rusted
bars still keep you in or out, a place to lock up deserters
and threaten with drowning by inches

Nietzsche was here but no one recognized him

beneath the bridge graffiti holds the bridge high
what doesn't kill you makes you stranger
we'll sit on the bank and weave beetles and eggshells in our hair

a cloudburst could bust the banks
a civil war soldier lived in a cave there, ran a ferry across

is Lower River a street or a command?

by the rivers of Don I sat down
and obstructed
the bike path,
cross me with your tire treads,
cormorant don't care, flies straight down
the centre of the water
and starlings in a silver maple know everything,
they won't charge for their gossip, they're no
better than they should be, listen

who's last beside the river who's lost a river?

against flooding and invading gadwalls
asters and goldenrod against apocalypse rocks
against ruin against a gull against traffic

let me out of this deadly nice city with
its red rockets and garrison condo mentality I'm
the most dangerous woman in America
I'm the deported lark of the Soviet ark
high priestess of anarchy
inspiration of assassins
editor of *Mother Earth*
I menace the population with free
milk for kids and my mugshot in white
blouse and pince-nez
to the daunting belongs the future
take my photo in a black T-shirt
and Google glasses
it behooves an agitator to dance on
her grave insignificance

JANE AND THE MONSTERS FOR BEAUTY, PERMANENCE, AND INDIVIDUALITY

after Duane Linklater

By the Don, beneath the bridge, gargoyles brought to earth, scale-model dragons and angels of revisionist history, beasts of Bay Street brought low and eye to eye with ideology and staghorn sumac, monsters of decolonial gravity watching Edward VII, Emperor of India, thrown into the river. Cast a cold concrete eye and a leg to boot. Well, I never. But Jane has, and won't mind telling you: trash floats and so does empire.

JANE, TRUTH, AND RECONCILIATION

Who tips their cap
italism to her
as they pass. Who signs on the dotted
line between panic and
panopticon. Property is
theft, Jane knows

perfectly well. Stolen
land sticks to the souls
of her feet. Jane used to lie
for a living; she had it down pat
riarchy, at its beck and col
onialism. Jane's a live wire
reckoning. Jane's recon
naissance is not recon
ciliation, not for want of wishing
which never made anything so.

She prizes her sorry state
sleeping rough because in an unsorry state
that humblebrags their
equal parts
con and quest,
asphalt won't absorb runoff
and an apology isn't worth
the paper it's not written on.

JANE, COUNTING DOWN

I'm a world
champion eraser; rubbed out
a house, a yard, egg beaters and
mixing bowls and lamps but all
I've set in motion are fantasies of fantasies
of peace. I wanted to
expunge myself, luxurious: I
debited my account to nil, threw
a lit match over my shoulder as I kicked
the door shut with my heel
and walked away. *Whoosh*
ka-boom. I never
met a border vacuum I wouldn't
puncture, a river I wouldn't
stand by for further instructions.
This is a test this is only
a test I am mobile and *alive alive oh*
in the place where so
many were killed.

FERN'S PRONUNCIATION GUIDE

MMIW is not
pronounced
mew. It could be
pronounced
me-you.
Or me-you-gee:
all those girls.

Enough talk.
The house is on fire.

JANE IN THE CHTHULUCENE

Grief's a strange
caffeine. Wide awake in
the carbon filter
imaginary, Jane might
join everything. Ragged,
lean-minded, livid.

FERN AND JANE DISCUSS THE QUEEN

If She's sleeping
outside tonight, we can lend Her
a Hudson's Bay blanket.

JANE'S CALL TO ACTION ON THE HUMBER BAY BRIDGE

I swear and make firm by the clapping
of my hands, I have faintfully
observed the law:
insurance means never
having to say your story. I sold
fear of the future and poured
vinegar on your grief, calculated
the cost of an arm or a leg,
totted up a partial
payout, smiled as I cut you
a cheque.

I swear and make firm by
the slapping of my thighs that I own
my lies of dividend, all the times I looked
you in the eye and said *God forbid.*
Sign here, selling you
FOMO, dying, losing.

I will fulfill my duties as a citizen of
rebar and birch, blister and corn,
winter on the grates proving I'm not
a garbage bag. Purchase Number
Thirteen, in the place where
trees stand in water and
on this bridge across
the bay, I see Tkaronto as

the definition of carrying
place, ten miles square or unsquare,
ten miles everywhere
down the portage route,
forever Yonge, world's longest
scream as long as grass is green.

JANE TALKS WITH THE BISHOP OF ROME ABOUT RECOMMENDATION 58

I met the Bishop on the road
allowance and much said he.
And I
waited. I folded my breasts flat.
Exactly why
is repentance for everyone
else to try?

He said *heavenly mansion,*
foul sty and *apologies*
are not
expansions
and *fair or foul, I can't see*
issuing another: the Irish were
enough. For nothing can be

sold quite like excrement
and if you buy that,
I've got
a wheelbarrow you can rent.
Your Eminence I said.
Your Cruelty. Your Intent.

Thought so.

JANE AND THE DANCERS IN ST. ALBAN'S SQUARE

I can tell the madmen's-morris dancers from
the dance. I'm a nixed minx cheered by perverse realities.

Get your knees up; let's jig away our fraternal wrecking
crew. A good mazurka rattles a lot of cages

if you do it right. Whisk me through the high voltage
gates of Elysium. You know me, unimpeded.

Jacobs's ladder, the roseway, sports blooms as heavy
and regular as a period. I am tortoise;

I am hare. A woman, to be mobile, needs 10,000
steps a day and a paradox of her own. Zeno

does everything by halves. My stone pillow
darling, meet me by the road that you

stopped in its tracks. Love like the teeth of
dandelions. Love, like all things, remains in sod.

the Grass Widow of Moss Park
the Swineherd of St. John's Ward
bona fide Viaduct Diva
our Myriad Mistress
our Everlasting Broad with a View

Jane lets the river answer
that it's always been her cover

JANE'S GATHERING

Furies boil beneath my skirts
and banshees in my gloves. A little
burlesque never hurts.

Unbutton and bring
the bridge to port.

By the stripping of these thumbs,
something winged
this way comes.

A woman in pain will forget to be kind or
clean. Probe the folds and ripples of her

cerebrum, her brain floating like a large grey
plum in a crater full of spring runoff. Walk local,

think lobal. When the road rains down
stone by pitted stone, when the bullhorn

roars, open the screw-top of her skull, reach in
and squeeze her cerebellum, dangling

scrotal above the intimate maze of
cognition. Under pressure, apply doubt.

Reaper, you're grim as promised. Your black robe
precedes you in this village of small huts. I'm a prisoner
with an agenda, with a tongue as curved as your scythe.
I'll sleep coughly in your harms.

I am fierce, bone dog, your paw between my teeth.

Apotheosis means getting high. Canonize me behind the
Wing On Funeral Home, sanctify me by the Bata Shoe
Museum. I put the *ain't* in saint. Tell Fern I'm
everynowhere.

Bastard rack of ribs, help me stand for this last lesson in
skirt-lifting. If I can't dance macabre, I don't want to be a
part of your world-class city.

*

Fury homing.
Ordinary shrug.
Hard by, our device.

Fury shrug. Homing
device, by hard
ordinance.

Hard shrug, Fury
device. Homing,
ordinary.

JANE'S DANCE

head back, arms up, she begins to spin
and she's slow, and who's to say
if monsters shook their heavy

Harryhausen heads, but she picks up speed
as bees swerve up from the laces
of her boots, June bugs leap

from her hair, crows call
from where they roost by the hundreds
before sunset in High Park

and cormorants complete
their beshitting of the harbour
and fly straight at the moon,

salmon swimming up the Humber sprout
wings and turn into sewer pigeons,
banshees small as swamp sparrows

howl as Jane spins fast enough to disappear
into a dust devil, a vortex of sidewalk
salt and newspaper

on the corner of Chester and Danforth,
grit in your eye,
a public woman

FERN'S FRIDAY

Fern's floured hands drop
chunks of dough in oil.
Everyone eats it fast.

At two o'clock, Fern sees
the plate she set aside and
knows Jane has passed.

JANE, GATHERED

A public woman was never
a paltry thing; gather me
into what is. To come, to see

emperors all long asleep and naked.
Whole, cracked, we'll go far.
When I sing, I breathe the stars.

Do you find safety in the tomb?
I couldn't say.
Still I'll stay.

A WORD ABOUT JANE FROM THE FURIES

Her/e.

Slow death cannot be photographed
for the six o'clock news.[1] Let someone
have gathered her up before the stars
assembled coldly overhead:[2] a bad
daughter, a bad sister described
nonetheless as rigid of will[3] against
the rolling dark oncoming river she
raised bulwarks.[4] A memory barely
retrieved from a fire is (the past)
in its hiding place.[5] The sleepy drummer
who beat on our eyes with an old story,[6]
the rest-in-peace of the placental
coracle,[7] shame is the failure to belong
sufficiently to what is beloved:[8]
what a heavy candelabrum to be
borne.[9] When the local hit the trestle
everything trembled.[10]

1   Marge Piercy, "The Long Death"
2   Amy Beeder, "Yellow Dress"
3   Adrienne Rich, "For Ethel Rosenberg"
4   Denise Levertov, "Olga Poems"
5   Carolyn Forché, *The Angel of History*
6   Anne Sexton, "Sylvia's Death"
7   Amy Clampitt, "A Procession at Candlemas"
8   Arleen Paré, "Northern Gate"
9   Maxine Kumin, "On Hearing of the Death of Anne Sexton"
10 C. D. Wright, "Bent Tones"

WORDS ABOUT JANE FROM THOSE WHO KNEW HER

We honour Jane of the Sidewalk. Time is
stippled. We taste mint, we know pigweed.
When we walk, the night adds up.

Oh Mother of Mother of Mother's
mothers. She'll take our time. She'll take it
on the lam like any well-fed storm.

Days like this she spent as water.
She turned the genus of common into
sense. She kept her intel close.

Her foolishness closer.
In the feast of hucksterism, she knew
her way around nothing.

She counted her bean rows; there were
eight. She kept shtum. She drank concord.
She was never who we thought.

3. BLUESTOCKINGS AND OTHER DISASTERS

The bluestocking…sinks wherever she is placed, like the yolk of an egg, to the bottom, and carries the filth with her.
—William Hazlitt

THE BLUESTOCKING'S OPENING LECTURE

after Sonya Huber

There is no extra credit for the truth.
No points will be deducted for lying.

Rough words are allowed but first
pay attention to their shine. Lateness

is allowed because I've been that girl with
the problem. Lateness is not encouraged

because same. I know it is shocking
to be read after so much knocking.

I will ask you to work with metaphor. Do not
tear up the pea patch. Pain is allowed, but

it's not a currency. It is addicting
to be read. I will write the prescription;

don't make me your pusher. Let it be said
you may call me by name after you've read

two of my books. You may think this is elitist.
Please discuss, at length, with the person

sitting next to you. I love it when you turn
to each other and speak. I will be grinning

as you talk. Do not be alarmed. These are only
my teeth. This is only happiness.

I wake up in perversity and dress head to toe in ontology.

I wake up in the spiral dance and mix my guts with garters.

I wake up one morning with my organs united.

The bugs find me by afternoon and make me one of them.

Being a goddess was overrated and underfunded. My
father did not save the garden for me.

I wake unworked like thread, my legs like scissors.

I wake on the mountaintop as the eagle consumes the last
of my liver.

I wake when the rabbits battle for supremacy, the chimpanzee
grasps the paradox of time travel, and the Einstein
woodpecker explodes.

Being a goddess was like being a meal: prepared,
consumed, shat out.

I used to have language intimacy issues, but now I wake
partial to vernacular on pancakes.

Hell may be other people, especially those promoting
their latest. Don't pretend you won't guard
the exits. Slipshod, shaking for sale, your name

spelled in a nebula of itch. Flash-mob humblebrag
like shit in a melting snowbank. The flesh dress
of authority rots and carnival-barker chaos

rules. It's a relief to hear that all the tests show
trace amounts of bile: the toxic haste dump. Rip-offs
and redneck irony read like quotations,

but they'll only bring you down. I'm a woman who
has attracted luscious, cruel advice, all
unasked for and most as mysterious as the secret

life of pants, but it all comes down to this lick of
inferno: you know that way you are?
Don't be that way.

BLUESTOCKING BLUES

I.

There's language in her
fist and she knows
how to punch the clock.

She starts you with her
mother tongue, sings
every tale packed tight

and carried north in a flour-sack
dress or wool pouch. Bring her
liniment for the muscles

of her broad and aching back.
Give room to her saudade,
bring her water:

some mansplainer's
callow words have maddened
every mother's daughter.

II.

At seven tonight, those
who listen will be those
who don't already know it all.

She doesn't know
how long she's got
to finish thinking, but

she has the mic
right now, and if you'd like
to ask, she will

answer. She will
listen to you at
length. Imagine that.

III.

Elm trees shed worms
and her notes
grow a black mould

no arborist will
touch. The longer she listens
to experts,

the more her body runs
out on her. Never enough
sleep and the baby she

did not bear bats
at her kidneys, not
caring if it kills the host.

Our subject does not
form a shadow
on the wall.

IV.

Forget column inches; you're worth
your weight in paper. Learn from

cautionary tales. It's easy to
spin out on bad planning.

Always find an alternate route.
Understand: success is speaking of

love and what you owe. Confidence is
a weasel released in the boardroom.

V.

She knows how *no* works.
She knows people with know-how.
It's her business to know.

It's a noxious business
but it brings the noise. It gives
her nodes, but you know

nodding goes both ways.
She knows which way is up.
It's a known fact. The truth is

I know and can't
know it alone, so she gets
to know it with me.

When no one knows no, no one
knows enough
to know. Call it

need-to-know nihilism.
She knows some things just so
I won't have to.

LOATHLY LADY

Climb up to the garret and
electrocute your sentence. Bone-sick
already, molars ringing, bra strap

twisted into a laidly worm on
your loathly shoulder. Someday
you're going to give up jagging

similes, someday you'll halt the grind
and clout of your body, someday
you'll break the rule of threes—

but not today. Sometimes
it all comes down to how fast you
can shovel water. Blinking does not

soothe your eyes and squinting brings
out the lizard in you. The world has
a bad habit of playing footsie with

you while wife and kids wait
in the minivan. You are too
old for this ship and you can hear

a high note like the yowl of
a trapped lynx or a train whistle:
it's a woman screaming. It's you.

MEAN

October's a mean season, ripped gown
next to scarred town's industrial park.
Raccoon by the road, cheek to grass,

body stilled by traffic. Parks are
not for playing. They are for walking
through, head up, alert. Path

bleak with mud and stale breath. Pass
through on the way to a pile of
bricks and mortgage. I thought if

I lived this long you'd find your way
back. I thought you'd be the same
pain in the neck, but here. The creek runs

like a nose. Blue jays shriek at
the nests of smaller birds. Stay dead.
It's grey as a brain here,

and there's still no word for us.

I can't tell the difference between the heron I saw at 8:00 a.m.
and the heron I saw at 11:00 a.m.

I hit a skunk as I drove home from a production of *King Lear*.
On the scale of Carolinian forest displacement, how many
skunks does it take? Reason not the need.

The section on Glory is the hardest to read. I'm unsafe at any
speed.

Bela Lugosi took morphine to dull the pain of his sciatica. Bela
was a handsome bastard. I can press a spot on my hip so hot it
could down a plane. I don't press it.

The object of my affliction can change my good diction from
bright to nearly dead.

I'm dogged—aren't you?—by truths too obvious to have traction.

There are forty degrees of misogyny between crone and Chronos.

Mobility is not motility. To be moved is not to move. How then
to sneak up on yourself.

The museum weight of a blue whale's heart is posted for public
consumption.

My mother always said that if I was sewing on the machine,
and the needle went through my finger, I should keep pushing
the fabric through.

I didn't ask about bone.

THE SEXUAL POLITICS OF BLUESTOCKINGS

It is a truth universally acknowledged that
a department in possession of a tenured position
must be in want of a bluestocking.

She tolerates no drive-by quoting.

She lets her blues do the stalking.

Are you now or have you ever been?
Does what you're wearing come in green?

She pulls herself up by her bluestraps.

If the bluestocking fits, wear it.

Every bluestocking learns how to run.

All happy bluestockings are alike,
but she doesn't know many.

THE COMMON CANADIAN BLUESTOCKING

(tibialis caeruluemus Canadensis)

She is distinguished by her colourful ruff in the winter months, ranging from cerise on BC's Lower Mainland to palest mauve on the Newfoundland coast. In the summer months, bluestockings range as far south as Chile and as far north as the Arctic. The archive ecosystems frequented by bluestockings are rapidly disappearing. Conferences and protest sites are still prime sighting areas, but watch carefully; years of poaching have made the bluestocking an expert at blending into her environment. Pro tip: as the weather warms, you may observe a distinctive crest of hair sticking up from her crown; she will be difficult to approach in this traditional marking period.

FROM *THE HISTORY OF BLUESTOCKINGS IN UPPER CANADA*

(Fragments of this text, unearthed from a basement in North Beynon, Ontario, describe a genealogy of bluestockings from European immigration to the stunt journalism of the late 19th century. Authorship is unattributed to date.)

Frag. I: Blue Arrivals

Arriving in the southwest region in 1805, they immediately established a homestead near the woollen mill where work and water was plentiful. The bluestockings worked at the mill in the day and argued by night. In summer, they wrote far into the evening in the long light by the riverbank; in winter, shortened days meant less reading time. By 1807, several bluestockings had trained as candle makers and had established a brisk trade in dyes with the local Onondaga people. This partnership was to last for many years, strengthened by the mutual understanding that a woman who smiles constantly must be deranged. (p. 15)

Frag. II: Gender Wars of 1812

A key moment in the history arose in 1813, when Laura Secord, aroused from her perusal of Samuel Richardson's novel, overheard plans for an attack on the British troops camped at Beaver Dams from American soldiers who were rifling her library. A twenty-mile walk to warn the British army was no problem for a woman as well-read as Secord. When she met Cayuga hunters on her way, she asked them, "Is *Pamela* satire? I cannot tell." They brought her to Lieutenant James F, the youngest brother of Charlotte FitzGibbon, the Defoe scholar and athlete who had been twice President of the Royal Order of Bluestockings, and little Jimmy was clever in his own right. He dressed carefully in sky-blue breeches and scarlet waistcoat to welcome Secord, understanding that her visit could mean his advancement among Niagara's most dedicated readers. (p. 67)

ARE YOU IN, GENIUS?

If we can't be geniuses together, can't sand
the rough bark and find the grain,
can't manufacture fleet utopias, can't flatten

our tongues to sing dissonant
harmony, can't zag
when everyone else

is zigging, when

everyone else is shouting *zag goddamn it*, if we
can't be savannah or desert
creatures together, then let's show our palms

when we applaud, let's scar our thighs
with punctuation tattoos, let's
recall every city we've ever visited where

someone we didn't know restored us whole
—the waitress in Sudbury,
the banker near Christmas Hill—before

grief pressed us like goslings imprinted
on hip waders, and we knew
genius kills, genius aspirates on vomit,

let's consider if we can't spark our synapses
in a shared fuse box with red breaker
switches, let's feed

each other, let's braid

our hair together into a rope
bridge that spans
the arm of the ocean that breaks between

our rocky islands, let's inch out on the rope bridge
and sway, let's fish for the cod
that swim through the narrow channel.

EMILY DICKINSON'S REPLY TO BILLY COLLINS

My life, a hood, a floated gun, a cosmic till,
say a Monday gone past identical,
I've dogstarred a stray. How I roar in nilling

woods and how I rake the sky
and how I smile such light to see.
Did She who made the ham make me?

The valley's sudden glow,
Vesuvius at home;
volcano genius knows its own.

Let pleasure swim through the net;
let rage down from the rafters, set
like a chair on a pulley. When at night

I guard my head, I know:
the eider duck a steep pillow,
neither fuck shared with foe.

I'm deadly. None stir the pot a second time
when I play my fingers or elastic thumb.
Bid the women and their drummers come.

She who talks with her hands lives
stronger than fire. You have a brief
day to thrill me—roll up your sleeves.

THE LOVE SONG OF VIVIENNE HAIGH-WOOD

Let us go then, you and I,
where your archives are spread out
against the sky, like a mental patient
electroconvulsed against her will.
Oh do not say *Who is it*? I think
you know. I've come to visit.
I'm in my black beret and cape. Have
you erased me on the first try?
Among the women, there I lie.

I am not Sarah Bernhardt
though was meant to be.
The eternal Footman winks at me.
I have the diurnal Flu. Consider,
I was once handsome and tall as you.
Vulgar, though: my tongue of flame
would not cease to flicker. Fathom
blame between two and five:
no one has yet returned alive.

Mornings, evenings, dark spittoons, you
measured out your wife in bleak lampoons.
Oh, do not look so miserable.
Your conceit is not metaphysical.

And how should I begin?
Something's screwy in St. Louis.
Unoriginal sin.

In the room the Faber men come and go
and rub their muzzles like gigolos
or yellow smoke against the snow.
Time for you and time for me
and a hundred indiscretions that

indecision would foresee.
I would have shared Bertie
with you, each to each.
Do you dare? Can you reach?

I disturbed the universe. I presumed.
I reversed the minute that you tuned.
I am Lady Lazarus come back
from the dead to tell you all
it would have been worth it. After
all. This is what I meant.

My father was a landlord. Yours a brick.
My menstrual blood made you sick.
A girl in a punt. A bag of ferrets
round your neck. A palpable prick.
Fear of death by water. Virginia never
liked me: she printed your poetry
and called you hole-and-cornerish.
I would have bitten her
back for you.

But you would not swell a progress. You were
never glad to be of use. You would not
bestow one patronizing kiss.

Tiresias knows: I have foresuffered all. Your next
wife took my letters. What
did you say to my brother? He
swears I am as sane as he. HURRY UP
PLEASE ITS TIME. Finsbury Park's
a fine and restless place.

I linger in the chambers of my cell. Human
voices mistake me for your blank pages.

1) Ode

Let us now praise the Sweet Songstress of Saskatchewan.
She writes but she'll get over it eventually. A cow is not a muse.
She's got ideas above her station. What could a farm girl know
    about seasons?
She's so stupid she thinks the Romans conquered Saskatchewan.
She's so stupid she thinks she can translate German from a
    dictionary.
She's so stupid she doesn't know her best friend was doing it
    with everyone.
She's so stupid she thinks Regina is the big city. She thinks
    Wascana Lake is real.
She's so stupid she doesn't understand that travelling with a
    man meant letting him fuck her.
She's so stupid he fucked her anyway.
We laughed when she did not want to talk about the trip
    afterward.
We slapped our knees and howled. Let us poke her. Let us hold
    our sides.
Let us remember her death from mercury poisoning and call it
    the cherry on top.
Let us plow her under.
She's so stupid she can't even die right.

The Sweet Songstress knows her way around a cocktail.
Three times the poet laureate, she is not what you expect.
She hands you a gin and tonic in her apartment in Saskatoon.
"Ice makes the drink!" she calls to you from the sideboard.
She drinks two to your one and shows no ill effects.
She likes Jack Kennedy and wants to see Diefenbaker appoint
    more female cabinet members.
Miss Binks won't be accused of putting on airs. You try but
    can't call her Sarah.
Ellen Fairclough was acting Prime Minister for two days in
    February 1958, she says.
She tells you about her trip to New York City.
She stayed at the Barbizon at Lexington and 63rd
and dined at the Old Russian Bear with her American agent.
She's secretive about the new manuscript.

3) Sarah Binks Plans a Mock Wedding to Be Performed at the 25th-Anniversary Party Honouring the Marriage of Mathilde and Steve Grizzlykick, 1957

Sarah's writing the script and casting the wedding party.

Mathilde is Sarah's biggest fan. And best friend before she married.

Ole will make the best bride, ropy muscles in white tulle.

Henry Welkin, bridesmaid. He'll want some punchlines but Sarah will see about that.

A photo of Rover to serve as flower girl.

One of the older Schwantzhacker sisters as groom; doesn't matter which.

As father of the bride, Jacob Binks, fresh from his held-over engagement keeping poachers off his quarter section. He won't let anyone else touch the shotgun.

Sarah will play the minister and commit the two to another twenty-five years. She will urge all assembled to witness in the church basement what was begun in the meadow.

Nearly beloved, we are garnered here today in the sight of Gord to join in holy macaroni. Dearly beleaguered, if any among you abject to the joking of this woman and this morn, spit now or furthermore hitch your piece.

THE JUSTESS

after Borges

A woman who lets the chickens into the garden.
She who craves an hour of silence.
She who takes pleasure in tracing a dress pattern and
    running it up on the machine.
Two waitresses playing, in a café downtown, a grinning
    game of gin.
The baker of tarts, adding raspberries to crust.
The poet who reads this page with generosity, though it
    may not please her.
A woman and a man who read all of *By Grand Central
    Station I Sat Down and Wept.*
She who strokes a sheet smooth while wearing a polyester
    uniform.
She who speaks calmly about a wrong done to her.
She who is grateful for the existence of bell hooks.
She who sees when others are right and sees when she is.
These. Their loveliness in creases.

Knob mentality is a cesspool
if you're hip-deep in the luxury
of being misunderstood. Arrange
the squash as best you can.

Wade all life backward.

Two kinds of apples: pink ladies,
northern spies. The only time I like
anything is two weeks after it's over.
The fish is whittled clean.

Its source runs too far ahead.

Horn of plenty, spilling: a thousand
monkeys, and gullible is not
in the dictionary. Jolts of pain have
already churned me to butter.

The satisfactory emphasis is on revolving.

A grapeshot hare, neck lolling. When he
tells you he's uncreating himself into
existence, it's a relief to tag the thought
control centre of the universe.

Don't send steadily.

Cézanne's oranges: pick up a crate.
Write your grocery list in indelible
pencil and cruise the shelves for
only the finest in radiant tortellini.

To give heat is within the control of every human being.

A small brace of partridge. Salmonberries.
Winter's finally done, and you with it.
It's April, the weed catalogue's here.
Braid the bread; paint the leeks green.

After you know me, I'll be no one.

A SCOLD BRIDLES

I am the most interested person in
the world and that's not just my curiosity
talking. Pleasure is its own
prescription and you should never trust
a drunk man doing an imitation
of his father. Humblebragging
that you never finish books is
neither humble nor a brag,
though you're right to be
suspicious: a fool can always
find another fool to admire him.
When we name animals after
celebrities, we disappoint both.

Bit and bridle at half-truths. Archive
this. Now burn it. Now bury it.
Now say you don't know
what I'm talking about. That's history
and another fine
dress you've gotten us into.
A palindrome will prove the way is yaw.
The quiet to which you were accustomed
has now become a roar.
Insomnia takes practice, due to
the kinetic energy of the falling abject.
Nest cup. Next up. I never met
a rhetoric of excess I didn't like.

When you traffic in falsehoods,
rev the engines.
Leave shoes all over the house
for fast escapes.
Luna moths are not lunar modules, though
the personal is heretical: ephemera

merges with dementia.
I'll never be your
beast of burden of proof; it only hurts
when I scoff.

But if there were two of me, who
would you ignore first? When the natural
order of things fucks us all, it's time
to re-chaos the phylum. Listen, it's none
of your business what the dog is thinking,
and you are not at all who
we're cooking for.

Those who can say *ranger station*
without thinking of Yogi Bear
will be asked to recuse themselves.
When she met Mr. Rogers, Koko
called his cufflinks
flowers. Wolves have
kind eyes and intelligent
parasites. The power
ballad takes no prisoners, so
we're going to crow this place
wide open. Please press
your soul flat enough to slide
beneath the door.

A weed blows in the field of inquiry.
Ideas are an invasive species and
dumbfounding is a tricky
business, think you very much.
Where is the choice coming from?
No revolution begins without
a bender. Irony: now
fortified with real iron.
I like a little lemon in my veins.

REQUIEM

Dear iris, dear eye, dissolve
this favour, test David with
Sybil. Tremors are the future

and judges strict as vultures,
so roll up your sleeves. Numb death,
nature a creature reborn,

televangelists love. Free us
from the melodrama of continence:
nothing from nothing. Remand

what all withhold and say
what lives our fathers' Rotary Clubs
secured us: Rex Murphy, delirium

tremens, Majestic Savings and
Loan. Pity their fonts and
write this down: cheese pie,

cherry, add it up, a living cause
for leaving, forms of sedition.
Passing redemption like

a storefront, Jane's crossing
the bridge to look back
on the work we made. Let

us make of our shoes the best
judge: tax our toenails, our day's
ration of shine. Forgive us our

rays, our common shelves
because we kneel on this
riverbank, resolve

our exhaustive souls with
these uncivil syllables.
No dignity in a précis: say

it all, there's no bonus
for this year's ignoramus.
Between births, we predict.

Sequester our heads, dextrous
make our birches to
trip up evil, acrid flame and

bitter mouths inclined
to gold and the compline's
quarter turn to a contrite cure.

Lacrimose say we all, and resurge
upon favour: new jury, new urge.
So because it goes, lady: cherry

or cheese pie, dominatrix,
wary, varicose, blistered,
give us rest.

"Flâneuserie" uses Michel de Certeau's "Walking in the City" as an intertext.

"Sybil Elegies" began with, and is variously allusive to, Dennis Lee's 1972 *Civil Elegies and Other Poems*. I wanted to write about a young woman's experience of urban citizenship, or how to "throe like a girl," using Lee's text as a template. The numbered elegies in this book are in conversation with—but don't necessarily correspond to—Lee's numbered elegies.

"Jane Walks" picks up the many iterations of the "Crazy Jane" figure as written by many poets, but most specifically in eight poems by W. B. Yeats. In addition, this section takes as its guiding spirit Jane Jacobs, the great urban critic who moved to Toronto in 1968 and lived in the Annex neighbourhood from 1971 to 2006. My Jane is not Jacobs, but I hope she would have liked this version of "eyes on the street." "Jane Meets W. B. Yeats" is a rewrite of Yeats's "Sailing to Byzantium." Lisa Robertson's "Proverbs of a She-Dandy" influenced "Lucky Jane, Leaky Object" and "Jane, Rover." Parts of "Jane, Truth, and Reconciliation" were inspired by Eve Tuck and K. Wayne Yang's "Decolonization is not a metaphor." "Jane's Call to Action" considers Recommendation 94 of the Truth and Reconciliation Commission's Calls to Action. "Jane's Dance" modifies lines from Yeats's "Among School Children." "Jane and the Monsters for Beauty, Permanence, and Individuality" refers to Cree artist Duane Linklater's sculptures on the Lower Don Trail, installed in September 2017. "Jane Talks to the Bishop of Rome about Recommendation 58" works with Yeats's "Crazy Jane Talks with the Bishop." "Jane, Gathered" alludes to "Crazy Jane and the Bishop."

Shout-out to my sisters in contemporary bluestockingship: long may we read. Hazlitt's quotation about bluestockings was found in Elizabeth Eger's *Bluestockings: women of reason from Enlightenment to Romanticism*. "Emily Dickinson's Reply to Billy Collins" began with Dickinson's poem 754. "The Justess" responds to Jorge Luis Borges's "The Just." "The Bluestocking's Opening Lecture" grew from my annual reading of Sonya Huber's "Shadow Syllabus." "The Cyborg's Diary" is after Donna Haraway's "Cyborg Manifesto." All allusions to T. S. Eliot are intentional in "The Love Song of Vivienne Haigh-Wood," and Yeats's words madden every mother's daughter in "Bluestocking Blues." I've got Sarah Binks's back and her sandwich close to my heart. The italicized lines in "Still Life with Lorine Niedecker" are from the first three pages of Niedecker's Calendar Poems, also known as "Next Year, or I fly my rounds, Tempestuous."

A scold's bridle (also known as branks) appears to be a Scottish invention from the 17th century. It is a metal mask clamped onto the head of a woman to stop her from speaking, and one more way the Scots invented the modern world to which I say: fuck you, forebears. The "bridle" included a spiked metal piece that pressed down on the woman's tongue and caused great pain if she spoke. The use of the device spread to England and Germany and was employed until mid-19th century to control the speech of "scolds," women who spoke inconveniently or critically. The woman in the bridle could be led through town or tethered to a public post as a form of ritual humiliation. In North America, where ritual humiliation was monetized to power the production of indigo, cotton, and other colonizing cash crops, branks were used on enslaved people in 18th-century Virginia and elsewhere.

"Requiem" is a homophonic translation of the fifth section of the Latin requiem "Sequentia: Dies Irae."

THANKS AND ACKNOWLEDGEMENTS

A long time ago, after an especially lively class, Chris Fox suggested that I write some "uncivil elegies." The more I wrote about Toronto as an urban space, the more I thought about the land on which that city spreads and the land on which I live as a settler and treaty person west of there, on the traditional territories of the Neutral, Anishnaabe, and Haudenosaunee peoples and part of the Haldimand Treaty of 1784.

Thanks to the many people upon whom I rely for poetry talk—in person and online: Sonnet L'Abbé, Maureen Hynes, Mariam Pirbhai, Maureen Scott Harris, Ariel Gordon, Jane Eaton Hamilton, Shannon Maguire, Colleen Murphy, Madhur Anand, Sarah Tolmie, Pamela Mordecai, Tanja Saari Bartel, and Leena Niemela. Gary Barwin asked me several important questions that changed how I thought about Jane in the city.

Huge thanks to Jay MillAr and Hazel Millar at Book*hug for everything they do and to Cara-Lyn Morgan for her generous reading at a crucial stage. My fantastic editor, Laurie D. Graham, advised me with care and humour throughout. Stuart Ross brought his steady eye.

I am grateful to the editors of the venues in which these poems appeared in early form:

- Part of "elegy 5" as "Sybil Elegies" in *Lemon Hound*.
- "Words About Jane from Those Who Knew Her" appeared as "Jane: an introduction" in *The Rusty Toque*.
- "No Exit," "Jane at the Barricades," "Emily Dickinson's Reply to Billy Collins," "Pirate Jane and the Don River" and part of "elegy 4" in *Contemporary Verse 2*.

- "The Sexual Politics of Bluestockings" in *Public Poetics* (WLUP 2015).
- "The Justess" on the website *Canadian Poetries.*
- "Still Life with Lorine Niedecker," "Jane, City Cosmonaut," "Jane's Citifesto," and "Jane and the Dancers" in *Canthius.*
- Early versions of "Jane's Nightingale," "Jane Meets W. B. Yeats," "Lucky Jane, Leaky Object," "The Rapture of Clever Jane," and "At the Yeats Exhibit at the National Library in Dublin" in *Understorey.*
- "Mean" in *Gamut.*
- The *Sarah Binks* poems were written during a Visiting Fellowship at the University of Saskatchewan, supported by the Interdisciplinary Centre for Culture and Creativity. The poems were first published in *Prairie Fire.*

"Are You In, Genius?" is for John Roscoe.
"Loathly Lady" is for my Garretians.
"Mean" is in memory of Wilf Gaidosch.

Tanis MacDonald is the author of several books of poetry and essays, including *Out of Line: Daring to Be an Artist Outside the Big City*. She is the co-editor of *GUSH: Menstrual Manifestos for Our Times* (2018) and the editor of *Speaking of Power: The Poetry of Di Brandt* (2006). Her book, *The Daughter's Way*, was a finalist for the Gabrielle Roy Prize in Canadian Literary Criticism. She is the winner of the Bliss Carman Prize (2003) and the Mayor's Poetry City Prize for Waterloo (2012). She has taught at the Sage Hill Writing Experience, and in 2017 won the Robert Kroetsch Teaching Award from the Canadian Creative Writers and Writing Programs. Originally from Winnipeg, she teaches Canadian Literature and Creative Writing at Wilfrid Laurier University in Waterloo, Ontario.

Manufactured as the first edition of *Mobile*
in the fall of 2019 by Book*hug Press

Edited for the press by Laurie D. Graham
Copy edited by Stuart Ross
Type + design by Ingrid Paulson

bookhugpress.ca